Contents

Some words are shown in bold, **like this**. You can find them in the glossary on page 23.

Why do we need water?

At home we need water for drinking and for cooking.

You have to drink water every day to stay healthy.

In the garden, we give water to plants to help them grow.

We also need water for washing ourselves and our clothes.

Where do we get water?

We get most of our water from rain.

When rain falls, some of the rain flows into streams and rivers.

6

dam

We store water from rivers in lakes called **reservoirs**.

A **dam** stops the water flowing away.

How does water get to my home?

pipe

Water travels to your home along pipes.

Giant pipes carry the water from **reservoirs** to towns and cities.

8

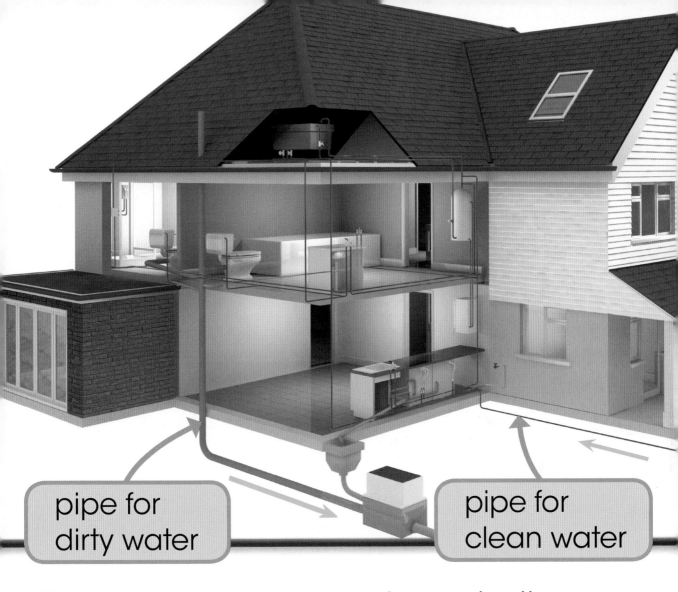

pipe for
dirty water

pipe for
clean water

The giant pipes carry water under the
ground along the streets.

Narrow pipes take the water from the giant
pipes into homes.

Why does water come out of a tap?

Powerful **pumps** push the water along the pipes to your home.

When you open a tap, this push makes water flow out of the tap.

leak

Sometimes a water pipe gets a leak.

This can happen if water in the pipe freezes into ice and splits the pipe.

Where does dirty water go?

Dirty water from your home goes down special pipes called drains.

The drains from each home join big underground pipes called **sewers**.

Sewers carry the dirty water to a **water treatment works** to clean it.

The cleaned water then goes into a river or to the sea.

Why does dirty water need to be cleaned?

Dirty water is dangerous to drink or to swim in.

If a person drinks or swallows dirty water, they can become very ill.

dead fish

Dirty water often has harmful chemicals in it.

The chemicals can harm the animals and plants that live in rivers and the sea.

How much water do we use at home?

A washing machine uses about 50 **litres** of water for each load of washing.

That is enough to fill 50 large bottles of lemonade!

Activity	Amount of water
Taking a shower	30 litres
Taking a bath	80 litres
One toilet flush	6 litres
Washing machine load	50 litres
Running the tap	10 litres a minute

This table shows how much water we use for different things.

Each day, a person uses between 100 and 200 litres of water at home.

Can we use as much water as we want?

reservoir

When the weather is very dry, the amount of water in **reservoirs** goes down.

Then we need to be even more careful not to use more water than we need.

Sometimes, an underground pipe bursts and no water comes out of your taps.

Then water has to be brought to your street in water trucks.

How can we use less water?

You can use less water in many ways.

One way to save water is to turn the tap off while you brush your teeth.

20

water butt

A **water butt** collects rainwater that flows off your home's roof.

You can use this water to water plants or clean your car, instead of tap water.

21

Keep a water diary

Copy this table onto a sheet of paper.

Make a tally of how many times your family uses water in one day. Do you think you could have saved any water?

Activity	Litres of water	Tally
Toilet flush	6 |卌 |||
Shower	30	|||
Bath	80	||
Washing machine	50		
Dishwasher	15		
Running a tap	10 (each minute)	卌 卌

Glossary

 **dam** thick wall that holds water in a reservoir

 **litre** measure of the space that some water takes up. A large bottle of fizzy drink holds one litre.

 **pump** machine that pushes water from one place to another

 **reservoir** lake that holds water for homes

 **sewer** large pipe for carrying away dirty water and waste from drains

 **water butt** large barrel used for catching and keeping rainwater

 **water treatment works** place where dirty water is cleaned

Find out more

Books

The Tale of One Well: Water (Big Picture), Sarah Levete (A&C Black, 2011)

Water (Reduce, Reuse, Recycle), Alexandra Fix (Heinemann Library, 2008)

Websites

www.yorkshirewater.com/education-and-learning/virtual-tour.aspx
Find information about where we get water and how water is cleaned, on this website by Yorkshire Water.

Index